Writing With Diligence

Written by
Geoffrey T. Garvey
and Michael J. McHugh

Christian Liberty Academy
Handwriting Program

Written by Geoffrey T. Garvey and Michael J. McHugh

Cover design by Robert Fine

Layout and graphics by **imagineering studios, inc.**

Printed with permission by

Christian Liberty Press
502 West Euclid Avenue

Arlington Heights, IL 60004

www.christianlibertypress.com

ISBN 978-0-9618275-1-9
        0-9618275-1-3

Printed in the United States of America

Contents

Aa Bb Cc Dd

Ee Ff Gg Hh

Ii Jj Kk Ll Mm

Nn Oo Pp Qq

Rr Ss Tt Uu Vv

Ww Xx Yy Zz

1 2 3 4 5

6 7 8 9 10

Preface

This is the second text in the Christian Liberty Academy series in handwriting. We remind you that one key to teaching success is reducing frustration in both parent and student. A wise teacher will not fail to take into account the maturity of the children so they can enjoy their handwriting activities without constant boredom or extreme fatigue.

Learning can and should be fun. The staff at Christian Liberty Academy has taken care to design each lesson to fit the attention span of the average primary student. Patience, prayer, and persistence are indispensable for success in teaching primary handwriting. It is very important for instructors to realize that extra drill work (on the blackboard and practice paper) must be assigned for each and every concept in the textbook. In addition, have the students practice each exercise before writing their work in the book.

In the first and second grade, the student's careful attention to the component strokes of letters becomes important. This is the reason the letters are taught in stroke groups rather than in alphabetical order. Nevertheless, special attention must be spent on developing a good oral and visual memory of alphabetical order. Alphabet flash cards and songs are convenient ways to establish this critical skill.

Both gross and fine motor skills are involved in handwriting. Certain abilities are generally found at this beginning level of development:

1. Good control of pencils, scissors, buttons, and zippers.

2. Ability to follow a series of spoken or written directions.

3. Ability to trace lines.

4. Ability to draw figures such as circles and squares.

5. Ability to distinguish between proper and improper spacing.

This text contains activities to develop and maintain the above skills.

Good handwriting is an essential skill of expression and communication. Time spent on handwriting is well spent. May the God of all grace help you develop students who will desire to write legibly and attractively for the glory of God.

Michael J. McHugh

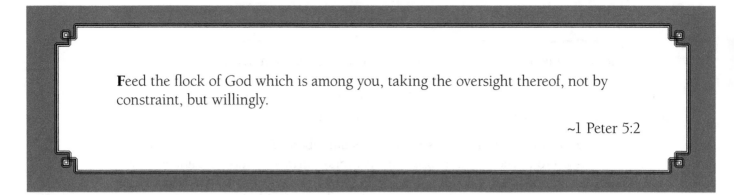

Feed the flock of God which is among you, taking the oversight thereof, not by constraint, but willingly.

~1 Peter 5:2

Introduction to Parents

In this text you will be asking your students to take more responsibility for their handwriting skills. You will be introducing vocabulary so that you and your students can use the same words to talk about how to write and areas for improvement. Some of the vocabulary (for instance, slanted line, clockwise circle) describes what to write and some (headline, midline) describes where. You will be asking your students to evaluate their own developing writing ability.

Before you begin, make sure your students have the proper readiness skills:

1. Can the students hold the pencil in a correct fashion?
2. Do the students recognize the difference in forms of letters and words?
3. Do the students appreciate handwriting as a means of communication?
4. Are the students reasonably able to copy a letter?

To improve fine motor skills and eye-coordination, make sure your students have ample opportunity to cut and paste, use paint brushes, draw with chalk on a board, create with clay, play ball, build with blocks, hammer pegs, and finger-paint. All these playful activities develop and strengthen the skill necessary for handwriting.

Proper forming of letters requires complete relaxation of all the muscles not directly involved in the act of writing: the fingers and wrist should be relaxed, not tense. The forearm should pivot on the elbow to direct hand and pencil along the horizontal line of the paper.

To help students get ready to write, they should be taught to:

1. Sit up straight, leaning forward slightly
2. Rest both arms on the desk
3. Keep both feet on the floor
4. Relax

Handwriting will improve if practiced every day. Fifteen to twenty minutes a day is sufficient at this grade level. If the student is improving at a slower pace than is reasonable, chances are that the student needs more time doing readiness activities first. Don't be tempted to increase handwriting practice time–when readiness skills are developed enough, the student will improve in handwriting skills most efficiently without being pushed.

Left-Handedness

Make sure your students are using the hand that is most natural for them. If you are unsure, watch to see which hand your student uses to reach for things, which foot starts a flight of stairs, which hand he uses to throw a ball, and with which hand the student has the best fine motor skills (coloring, inserting a key, picking up a coin). The hand that predominates is the hand to be encouraged. Remember that left-handed students will have a more difficult task, because the movement from left to right across the page is awkward for the left hand.

2

Proper Writing Posture

Some children write with their left hand. This picture shows how they should sit when they write.

Some children write with their right hand. This picture shows how they should sit when they write.

Some children write with their left hand. This picture shows how they should hold their pencil.

Some children write with their right hand. This picture shows how they should hold their pencil.

Some children write with their left hand. This picture shows how they should stand at the chalkboard.

Some children write with their right hand. This picture shows how they should stand at the chalkboard.

Connect the pictures with a line. Draw from left to right.

Connect the pictures with a line. Draw from left to right.

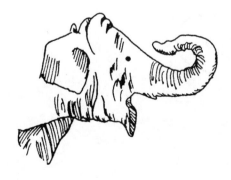 

Draw a line on the path from the girl to the ice cream cone. Try to stay in the lines.

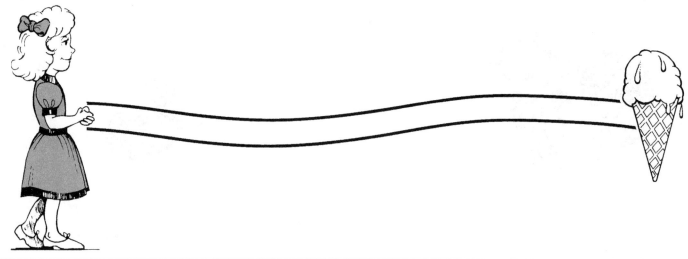

Draw a line on the path from Mary and Joseph to Bethlehem. Try to stay in the lines.

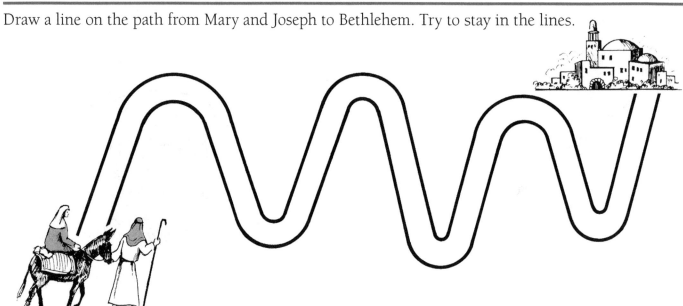

Draw a line on the path from the bird to the nest. Try to stay in the lines.

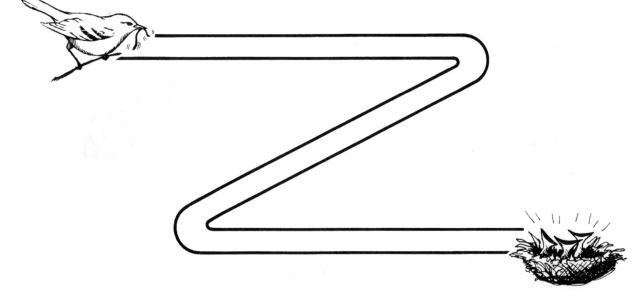

Clockwise

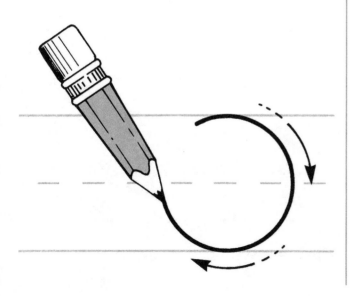

Counter-clockwise

Clockwise Circle

Start from the dot. Draw a circle up to the headline, down to the baseline, and then back to the starting dot. Go in the direction of the arrow.

Draw a clockwise circle.

Counter-clockwise Circle

Start from the dot. Draw a circle up to the headline, down to the baseline, and then back to the starting dot. Go in the direction of the arrow.

Draw a counter-clockwise circle.

Provide more practice on the chalkboard or on ruled paper, as needed.

Clockwise Semicircle

Start from the dot. Draw a semicircle down to the
baseline and then up to the midline. Go in the
direction of the arrow.

Draw a clockwise semicircle.

Counter-clockwise Semicircle

Start from the dot. Draw a semicircle up to the
midline and then down to the baseline. Go in the
direction of the arrow.

Draw a counter-clockwise semicircle.

Provide more practice on the chalkboard or on ruled paper, as needed.

Full Space

Start at the dot. Draw a straight line down from the headline to the baseline.

Draw a line.

Half Space

Start from the dot. Draw a straight line down from the midline to the baseline.

Draw a line.

Provide more practice on the chalkboard or on ruled paper, as needed.

Vertical Stroke Practice

Draw a straight line down from the headline to the baseline. There are some shaded lines to trace to get started.

Horizontal Stroke Practice

Draw a straight line on the midline. There are some shaded lines to trace to get started.

Slant Stroke Practice

Draw a slanted line down from the headline to the baseline. There are some shaded lines to trace to get started.

Provide more practice on the chalkboard or on ruled paper, as needed.

Punctuation
Period
Don't be too concerned with the precision of the children's concept of a sentence at the first-grade level. It is enough for the children to understand that a sentence is a complete thought.

The period is a dot we put at the end of a sentence where the sentence ends. The period is made on the baseline.

Question Mark
Begin at the dot just below the headline. Make a semicircle up to the headline down to the midline and continue from the midline almost to the baseline. Finish by making a dot on the baseline right under the straight line.

The question mark goes at the end of a question.
Draw a question mark. There are some shaded lines to trace to get started.

Comma
Begin by making a dot on the baseline and continue with a small semicircle under the baseline.

The comma is used to show a pause inside a sentence.
Draw a comma. There are some shaded lines to trace to get started.

Provide more practice on the chalkboard or on ruled paper, as needed.

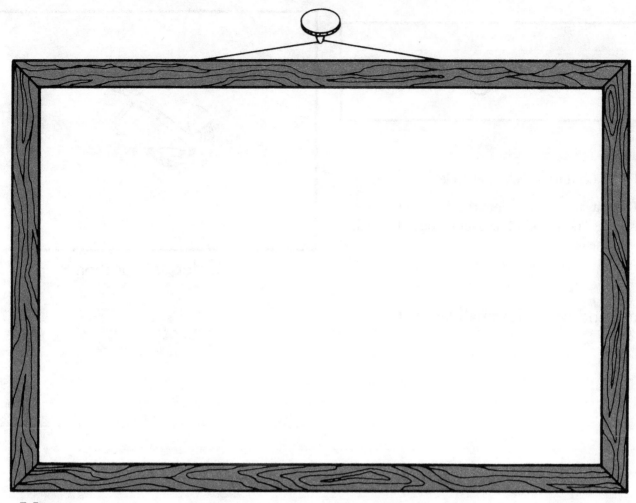

My Name

Draw a picture of yourself in the frame. Practice writing your name.

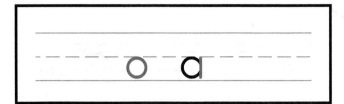

Instructions

1. Draw a counter-clockwise circle.

2. Draw a straight line from the midline to the baseline. The straight line should touch the right side of the circle

Color the anchor.

Trace and write the small letter **a**.

Write the letter **a**.

Provide more practice on the chalkboard or on ruled paper, as needed.

Instructions

1. Begin at the headline and draw a slanted line down to the left ending at the baseline.

2. Beginning at the start of the first stroke, draw a slanted line to the right ending at the baseline.

3. Draw a horizontal line just below the midline from the first stroke to the second stroke.

COLOR THE ANGEL.

Trace and write the capital letter **A**.

Provide more practice on the chalkboard or on ruled paper, as needed.

15

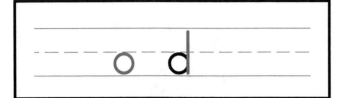

Instructions

1. Draw a counter-clockwise circle from the midline to the baseline.

2. Draw a straight line from the headline to the baseline. The straight line should touch the right side of the circle.

Color the dog.

Trace and write the small letter **d**.

Write the word **add**.

Write the words **A dad**.

Provide more practice on the chalkboard or on ruled paper, as needed.

16

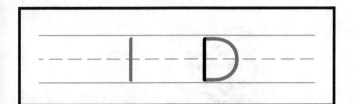

Instructions

1. Draw a straight line from the headline to the baseline.

2. Beginning at the start of the first stroke, draw a large semicircle to the baseline. The second stroke should end where the first stroke ended.

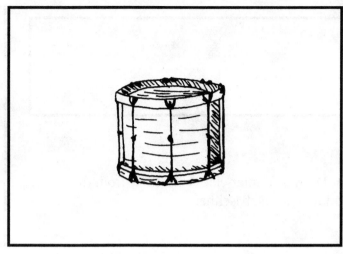

COLOR THE DRUM.

Trace and write the capital letter **D**.

Write the word **Dad.**

Write the sentence **Add, Dad.** Don't forget the period or the comma.

Provide more practice on the chalkboard or on ruled paper, as needed.

17

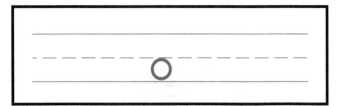

Instructions

1. Draw a counter-clockwise circle from the midline to the baseline.

Color the owl.

Trace and write the small letter **o**.

Write the word **odd**.

Write the words **Do add**.

Provide more practice on the chalkboard or on ruled paper, as needed.

18

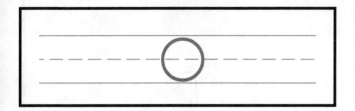

COLOR THE ONION.

Instructions

1. Draw a counter-clockwise circle from the headline to the baseline.

Trace and write the capital letter **O**.

Write the word **Odd.**

Write the words **O Dad.**

Provide more practice on the chalkboard or on ruled paper, as needed.

19

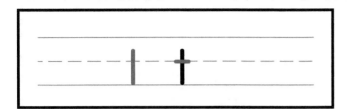

Instructions

1. Draw a straight line from halfway between the headline and midline to the baseline.

2. Draw a straight line on the midline. The straight line should cross the first stroke.

Color the truck.

Trace and write the small letter **t**.

Write the word **to**.

Write the sentence **Do a dot, Dad.** Don't forget the period.

Provide more practice on the chalkboard or on ruled paper, as needed.

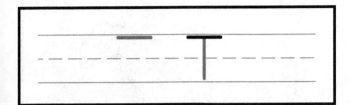

COLOR THE TREE.

Instructions

1. Draw a horizontal line on the headline.

2. Beginning at the middle of the first stroke, draw a straight line from the headline to the baseline.

Trace and write the capital letter **T**.

Write the word **Toad**.

Write the words **To Dad**.

Provide more practice on the chalkboard or on ruled paper, as needed.

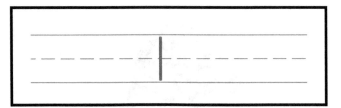

Color the lamb.

Instructions

1. Draw a straight line from the headline to the baseline.

Trace and write the small letter l.

Write the word **load**.

Write the words **A doll**.

Provide more practice on the chalkboard or on ruled paper, as needed.

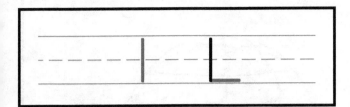

COLOR THE LION.

Instructions

1. Draw a straight line from the headline to the baseline.

2. Beginning at the end of the first stroke, draw a horizontal line on the baseline.

Trace and write the capital letter **L**.

Write the word **Lad**.

Write the words **Load a lot**.

Provide more practice on the chalkboard or on ruled paper, as needed.

23

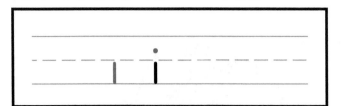

Instructions

1. Draw a straight line from the midline to the baseline.

2. Put a dot above the straight line.

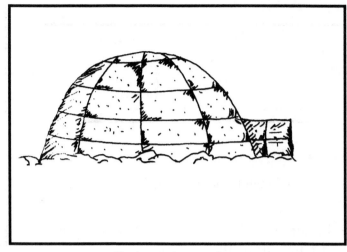

Color the igloo.

Trace and write the small letter **i**.

Write the word **lit.**

Write the sentence **Did Lot do it?** Don't forget the question mark.

Provide more practice on the chalkboard or on ruled paper, as needed.

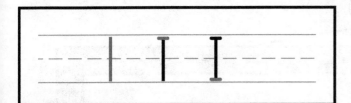

Instructions

1. Begin by drawing a straight line from the headline to the baseline.

2. Draw a short horizontal line on the headline. The horizontal line should cross the first stroke.

3. Draw a short horizontal line on the baseline. The horizontal line should cross the first stroke.

COLOR THE ICE CREAM.

Trace and write the capital letter I.

Write the word It.

Write the sentence I lit it. Don't forget the period.

Provide more practice on the chalkboard or on ruled paper, as needed.

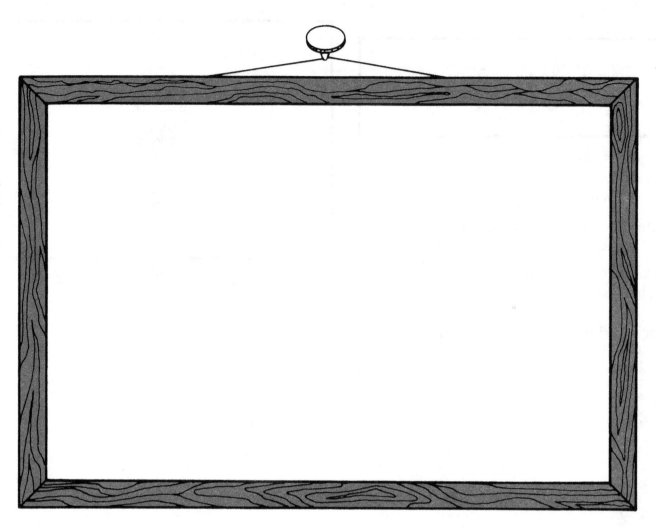

Here are some words you can make with the letters you have practiced: **add, at, aid, dad, do, did, doll, dot, toad, tall, till, lad, lid, load, lot, lit, laid, it, I**.
Use them to write a letter to a friend. Draw a picture in the frame to go with your letter.

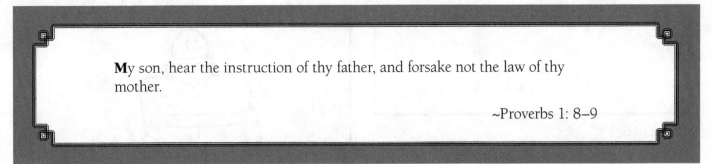

My son, hear the instruction of thy father, and forsake not the law of thy mother.

~Proverbs 1: 8–9

Teaching Notes

1. Am I setting a good example with my handwriting?
2. Am I praising the accomplishments as well as correcting the mistakes?
3. Am I providing a variety of activities to improve fine motor skills?
4. Am I encouraging the students to practice a small amount every day?

At the bottom of this page ask the students to critique their own handwriting. "What letters do you write the best?" "Which letters are the hardest?" Help the students to see how letters are the same and how they are different. Encourage the use of handwriting vocabulary. Focus your own attention on letters done well. After the students diagnose their own problem letters, provide ruled paper for practicing the problem letters.

Help your students discover these important rules in manuscript writing:

1. All letters begin at the top and move to the bottom.
2. All letters are made with straight lines and circles.
3. Letter parts are added from left to right. (**d** is **o** + **l**)
4. The first letter of a sentence or a proper name is capitalized.
5. Sentences have punctuation at the end.
6. Circle letters are close together, circle letters and vertical letters farther apart, and two vertical letters the farthest apart. First attempts for spacing between words can be the width of the child's finger. Over time the space should be reduced to the width of an **o**.

Make sure good manuscript form is well established before encouraging the use of cursive handwriting. Now help your students evaluate how they are progressing.

How Am I Learning?

Are you ready to write? Do your best work as you copy this sentence.
I did a lot.

Answer the following questions.	Circle	
1. Do all my letters slant in the same direction?	Yes	No
2. Am I shaping every letter correctly?	Yes	No
3. Am I making each letter the correct height?	Yes	No
4. Am I spacing letters evenly?	Yes	No
5. Am I leaving space between words?	Yes	No

Letters I write well:

Letters I need to practice:

27

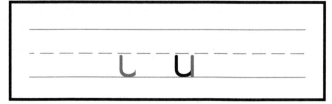

Instructions

1. Draw a straight line from the midline. Finish in a half circle at the baseline. The half circle should touch the baseline and finish just above the baseline.

2. Draw a straight line from the midline to the baseline. The straight line should touch the right side of the end of the half circle.

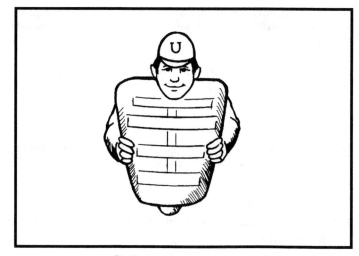

Color the umpire.

Trace and write the small letter **u**.

Write the word **dull**.

Write the words **A loud toad**.

Provide more practice on the chalkboard or on ruled paper, as needed.

28

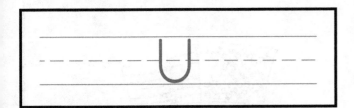

Instructions

1. Draw a straight line down from the headline to just below the midline.

2. Continue drawing a half circle down to the baseline. The half circle should touch the baseline and continue up to just below the midline.

3. Then draw a straight line up to the headline.

COLOR THE UMBRELLA.

Trace and write the capital letter U.

Provide more practice on the chalkboard or on ruled paper, as needed.

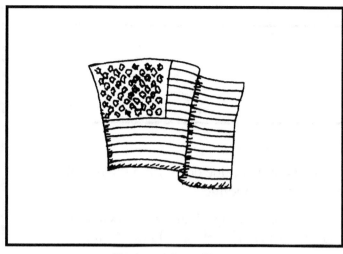

Color the flag.

Instructions

1. Draw a counter-clockwise half circle at the headline and finish in a straight line to the baseline.

2. Draw a straight line on the midline. The straight line should cross the straight line with the half circle.

Trace and write the small letter **f**.

Write the word **fl ood.**

Write the sentence **Lift a foot.** Don't forget the period.

Provide more practice on the chalkboard or on ruled paper, as needed.

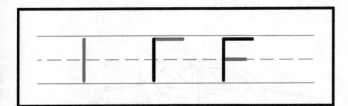

Instructions

1. Draw a straight line from the headline to the baseline.

2. Beginning at the start of the first stroke, draw a horizontal line on the headline.

3. Beginning on the first stroke, draw a shorter horizontal line on the midline.

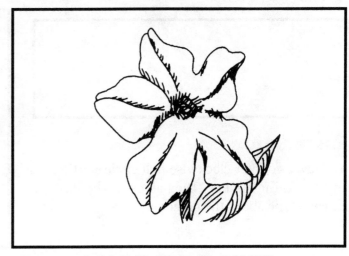

COLOR THE FLOWER.

Trace and write the capital letter **F**.

Write the word **Fall**.

Write the words **Full load**.

Provide more practice on the chalkboard or on ruled paper, as needed.

31

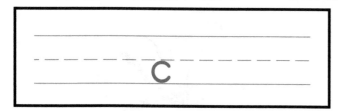

C

Instructions

1. Draw a counter-clockwise half circle starting just below the midline. The half circle should finish a little above the baseline.

Color the car.

Trace and write the small letter **c.**

C

Write the word **cute.**

Write the sentence **Dad cut it**. Don't forget the period.

Provide more practice on the chalkboard or on ruled paper, as needed.

32

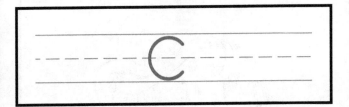

Instructions

1. Draw a counter-clockwise half circle just below the headline. The circle should finish a little above the baseline.

COLOR THE CHURCH.

Trace and write the capital letter **C**.

Write the word **Call.**

Write the sentence **Could Tad act loud?** Don't forget the question mark.

Provide more practice on the chalkboard or on ruled paper, as needed.

Instructions

1. Draw a counter-clockwise half circle starting halfway between the midline and the baseline. The half circle should finish a little above the baseline.

2. Draw a straight line halfway between the midline and the baseline. The straight line should connect the left side of the half circle to the beginning of the half circle.

Color the elephant.

Trace and write the small letter **e.**

Write the word **eat.**

Write the sentence **A collie ate a little food.** Don't forget the period.

Provide more practice on the chalkboard or on ruled paper, as needed.

Instructions

1. Draw a straight line from the headline to the baseline.
2. Beginning at the start of the first stroke, draw a horizontal line on the headline.
3. Beginning on the first stroke, draw a shorter horizontal line on the midline.
4. Beginning at the end of the first stroke, draw a horizontal line on the baseline.

COLOR THE EAGLE.

Trace and write the capital letter **E.**

Write the word **Eddie.**

Write the sentence **Ellie felt odd.** Don't forget the period.

Provide more practice on the chalkboard or on ruled paper, as needed.

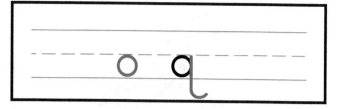

Instructions

1. Draw a counter-clockwise circle from the midline to the baseline.

2. Draw a straight line from the midline to the descender line, finishing in a half circle that just touches the descender line. The straight line should touch the right side of the circle.

Color the queen.

Trace and write the small letter **q**.

Write the word **quit.**

Write the words **A cold quilt.**

Provide more practice on the chalkboard or on ruled paper, as needed.

36

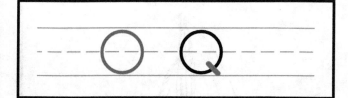

Instructions

1. Draw a counter-clockwise circle from the headline to the baseline.

2. Draw a short slanted line from left to right at the bottom of the circle. The line should pass through the side of the circle.

COLOR THE QUILT.

Trace and write the capital letter **Q**.

Write the word **Quote.**

Write the sentence **Queen Adelle called Tad**. Don't forget the period.

Provide more practice on the chalkboard or on ruled paper, as needed.

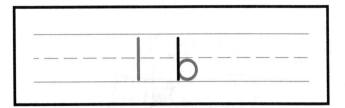

Instructions

1. Draw a straight line from the headline to the baseline.

2. Draw a clockwise circle from the midline to the baseline. The left side of the circle should touch the straight line.

Color the boat.

Trace and write the small letter **b**.

Write the word **bid**.

Write the sentence **Could a bulldog bite?** Don't forget the question mark.

Provide more practice on the chalkboard or on ruled paper, as needed.

Instructions

1. Draw a straight line from the headline to the baseline.
2. Beginning at the start of the first stroke, draw a half circle to the midline. The end of the half circle should touch the middle of the first stroke.
3. Beginning at the end of the second stroke, draw a half circle to the baseline. The end of the half circle should touch the end of the first stroke.

COLOR THE BIBLE.

Trace and write the capital letter **B**.

Write the word **Bill**.

Write the words **A blue Bible.**

Provide more practice on the chalkboard or on ruled paper, as needed.

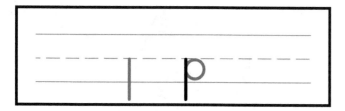

Instructions

1. Draw a straight line from the midline to the descender line.

2. Draw a clockwise circle from the midline to the baseline. The circle should touch the left side of the straight line.

Color the pineapple.

Trace and write the small letter **p**.

Write the word **pad.**

Write the sentence **Bob paid Callie**. Don't forget the period.

Provide more practice on the chalkboard or on ruled paper, as needed.

40

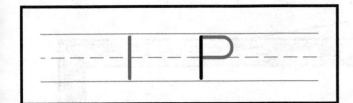

COLOR THE PUMPKIN.

Instructions

1. Draw a straight line from the headline to the baseline.

2. Beginning at the start of the first stroke, draw a half circle to the midline. The end of the half circle should touch the first stroke.

Trace and write the capital letter **P**.

P

Write the word **Paul**.

Write the sentence **Peter paid Paul**. Don't forget the period.

Provide more practice on the chalkboard or on ruled paper, as needed.

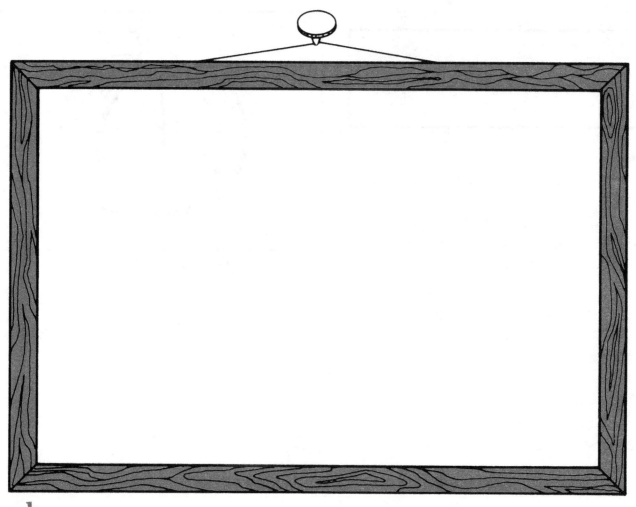

Food

Draw a picture of yourself eating your favorite food. Practice writing the title of your picture.

Teaching Notes

1. Am I setting a good example with my handwriting?
2. Am I praising the accomplishments as well as correcting the mistakes?
3. Am I providing a variety of activities to improve fine motor skills?
4. Am I encouraging the students to practice a small amount every day?

The ultimate purpose for handwriting is to express and communicate meaning. The desire to communicate will motivate your students to improve form and speed. Reversals of letters (backward letters) and some irregularity in size and form is expected, and nothing to express concern about. Remember a child likes to hoe a short row.

Help your students see the progress that has already been made. Keep a sample of the work from every week and bring it out occasionally to should how much improvement there has been. This is a powerful reinforcement of your verbal praise.

Show your students the many ways you use your own handwriting Write in manuscript when writing captions for their pictures. Encourage your students to learn to write their address and phone number. Help your students write the date, simple stories, and captions for their own pictures and charts.

Now help your students evaluate how they are progressing.

How Am I Learning?

Are you ready to write? Do your best work as you copy this sentence.
I pulled a blue quilt off the fat cat.

Answer the following questions.   Circle

1. Am I keeping all letters on the baseline?	Yes	No
2. Am I shaping every letter correctly?	Yes	No
3. Am I making each letter the correct height?	Yes	No
4. Am I spacing letters evenly?	Yes	No
5. Am I leaving space between words?	Yes	No
6. Am I capitalizing and using periods or questions marks?	Yes	No

Letters I write well:

Letters I need to practice:

☆
Begin at the headline and draw a straight line down to the baseline.

☆☆
Begin below the headline and make a forward semicircle up to the headline and back down in a slant to the baseline, finishing a horizontal line on the baseline.

☆☆☆
Begin below the headline and make a forward semicircle up to the headline and back down to the midline, then make another forward semicircle resting on the baseline.

☆☆☆☆
Begin at the headline and draw a straight line to the midline, then draw a horizontal line to the right on the midline. Begin at the headline and draw a straight line across the first stroke to the baseline.

☆☆☆☆☆
Begin at the headline and draw a straight line to the midline, then draw a forward semicircle resting on the baseline. Begin at the start of the first stroke and draw a horizontal line on the headline.

The Numeral 1

Color 1 star. Trace and write the numeral **1**.

The Numeral 2

Color 2 stars. Trace and write the numeral **2**.

The Numeral 3

Color 3 stars. Trace and write the numeral **3**.

The Numeral 4

Color 4 stars. Trace and write the numeral **4**.

The Numeral 5

Color 5 stars. Trace and write the numeral **5**.

(6 ⁻ 7 S8 °9 | |0

Begin at the headline and draw a slanted line past the midline, finishing in a counter-clockwise circle down to the baseline, up to the midline, and back to close the circle.

Begin at the headline and draw a horizontal line on the headline, then finish with a slanted line to the baseline.

Begin a counter-clockwise circle just below the headline, draw up to the headline, and down to the midline. Continue clockwise making a circle from the midline to the baseline, back up to the midline. Continue counter-clockwise circling up to just below the headline.

Make a counter-clockwise circle between the headline and the midline. Then begin at the headline and draw a straight line to the baseline, touching the first circle.

Make a numeral 1. Then draw a counter clockwise circle between the headline and the baseline.

The Numeral 6

Color 6 stars. Trace and write the numeral **6**.

The Numeral 7

Color 7 stars. Trace and write the numeral **7**.

The Numeral 8

Color 8 stars. Trace and write the numeral **8**.

The Numeral 9

Color 9 stars. Trace and write the numeral **9**.

The Numeral 10

Color 10 stars. Trace and write the numeral **10**.

Instructions

1. Draw a straight line from the midline to the baseline.

2. Draw a clockwise half circle starting on the straight line just below the midline. Finish in a straight line to the baseline.

Color the nail.

Trace and write the small letter **n.**

Write the word **nail.**

Write the sentence **Dan and I ate a bean**. Don't forget the period.

Provide more practice on the chalkboard or on ruled paper, as needed.

46

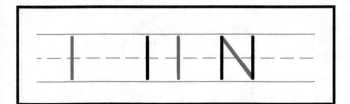

Instructions

1. Draw a straight line from the headline to the baseline.
2. Draw a straight line from the headline to the baseline about 3/8 of an inch apart.
3. Draw a slanted line left to right from the start of the first stroke to the baseline, ending at the base of the second stroke.

COLOR THE NURSE.

Trace and write the capital letter **N**.

Write the word **Nate**.

Write the sentence **Aunt Nan needed a cane**. Don't forget the period.

Provide more practice on the chalkboard or on ruled paper, as needed.

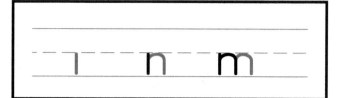

Instructions

1. Draw a straight line from the midline to the baseline.
2. Draw a clockwise half circle starting on the straight line just below the midline. Finish in a straight line to the baseline.
3. Draw another clockwise half circle starting on the half circle line just below the midline. Finish in a straight line to the baseline.

Color the monkey.

Trace and write the small letter **m.**

Write the word **model.**

Write the sentence **I am a model pupil.** Don't forget the period.

Provide more practice on the chalkboard or on ruled paper, as needed.

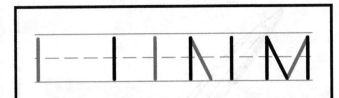

Instructions

1. Draw a straight line down from the headline to the baseline.
2. A half inch to the right of the first stroke, draw a straight line down from the headline to the baseline.
3. Draw a slanted line down to right from the start of the first stroke to the baseline.
4. Draw a slanted line down to left from the start of the second stroke to the end of the third stroke.

COLOR THE MOUSE.

Trace and write the capital letter **M.**

Write the word **Mailman.**

Write the sentence **Mother meant it.** Don't forget the period.

Provide more practice on the chalkboard or on ruled paper, as needed.

Color the rocket.

Instructions

1. Draw a straight line from the midline to the baseline.

2. Draw a clockwise half circle starting on the straight line just below the midline. The half circle should touch the midline and finish just below the midline.

Trace and write the small letter **r**.

Write the word **runner.**

Write the sentence **Mom rode in front.** Don't forget the period.

Provide more practice on the chalkboard or on ruled paper, as needed.

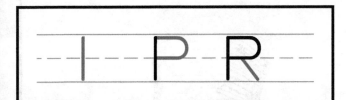

COLOR THE RABBIT.

Instructions

1. Draw a straight line from the headline to the baseline.
2. Beginning at the start of the first stroke, draw a half circle to the midline. The end of the half circle should touch the middle of the first stroke.
3. Beginning at the bottom of the half circle, draw a slanted line left to right to the baseline.

Trace and write the capital letter **R.**

Write the word **Rapid.**

Write the sentence **Ride in front near Mom, Rebecca**. Don't forget the period and comma.

Provide more practice on the chalkboard or on ruled paper, as needed.

51

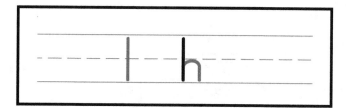

Instructions

1. Draw a straight line from the headline to the baseline.

2. Draw a clockwise half circle starting on the straight line just below the midline. Finish in a straight line to the baseline.

Color the hat.

Trace and write the small letter **h.**

Write the word **home.**

Write the words **Rachel and her children.**

Provide more practice on the chalkboard or on ruled paper, as needed.

52

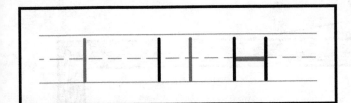

Instructions

1. Draw a straight line from the headline to the baseline.

2. Draw another straight line from the headline to the baseline.

3. Draw a horizontal line on the midline connecting the first and second strokes.

COLOR THE HOUSE.

Trace and write the capital letter **H.**

Write the word **Hail.**

Write the words **Horeb, a mountain of the Lord.**

Provide more practice on the chalkboard or on ruled paper, as needed.

53

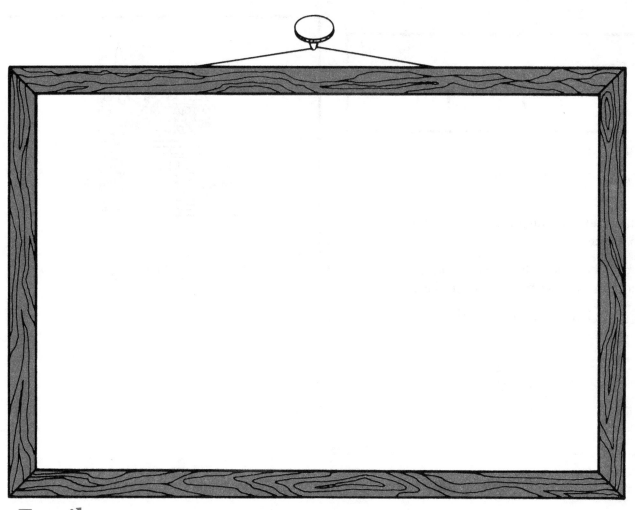

My Family

Draw a picture of your family in the picture frame. Practice writing their names.

> Fathers, provoke not your children to anger, lest they be discouraged.
>
> ~Colossians 3: 21

Teaching Notes

1. Am I setting a good example with my handwriting?
2. Am I praising the accomplishments as well as correcting the mistakes?
3. Am I providing a variety of activities to improve fine motor skills?
4. Am I encouraging the students to practice a small amount every day?

As your students improve in their handwriting skills, your attention will become less necessary. Your students should be starting to accept personal responsibility for appraising and improving their own handwriting. Remember, though, that good handwriting will not be achieved in a short time. Handwriting will still require some attention in high school as speed grows and personal style emerges.

Of course, even at the first-grade level each student has an individual style. Do not challenge this individuality unless it interferes with the ultimate purpose of communication.
Now help your students evaluate how they are progressing.

How Am I Learning?

Are you ready to write? Do your best work as you copy these sentences.
Randall made a fine hero. Mom and Dad are proud of him.

Answer the following questions.   Circle

1. Am I keeping all letters on the baseline?	Yes	No
2. Am I shaping every letter correctly?	Yes	No
3. Am I making each letter the correct height?	Yes	No
4. Am I spacing letters evenly?	Yes	No
5. Am I leaving space between words?	Yes	No
6. Am I capitalizing and using periods or questions marks?	Yes	No
7. Am I leaving extra space between sentences?	Yes	No

Letters I write well:

Letters I need to practice:

J j

Instructions

1. Draw a straight line from the midline to the descender line, finishing in a clockwise half circle that just touches the descender line and ends just above the descender line.

2. Put a dot above the straight line.

Color the jar.

Trace and write the small letter **j**.

j

Write the word **Jam.**

Write the sentence **Harold Jumped.** Don't forget the period.

Provide more practice on the chalkboard or on ruled paper, as needed.

56

Instructions

1. Draw a straight line from the headline to the midline, finishing in a clockwise half circle that touches the baseline. Stop just below the midline.

COLOR THE JEEP.

Trace and write the capital letter **J**.

Write the word **Jericho.**

Write the sentence **Jeremiah lamented for the Lord**. Don't forget the period.

Provide more practice on the chalkboard or on ruled paper, as needed.

57

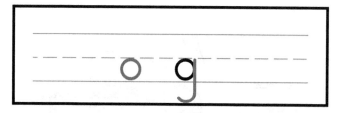

Instructions

1. Draw a counter-clockwise circle.

2. Draw a straight line from the midline to the descender line, finishing in a half circle that just touches the descender line and ends just above the descender line. The straight line should touch the right side of the circle.

Color the guitar.

Trace and write the small letter **g**.

Write the word **gentle**.

Write the sentence **Martin, get Bill a grape.** Don't forget the period and comma.

Provide more practice on the chalkboard or on ruled paper, as needed.

Instructions

1. Draw a counter-clockwise half circle starting just below the headline. The circle should finish at the midline.

2. Draw a horizontal line on the midline from the inside of the circle, ending at the end of the first stroke.

COLOR THE GRANDPARENTS.

Trace and write the capital letter **G**.

Write the word **Grandma.**

Write the sentence **Granddad got a gift**. Don't forget the period.

Provide more practice on the chalkboard or on ruled paper, as needed.

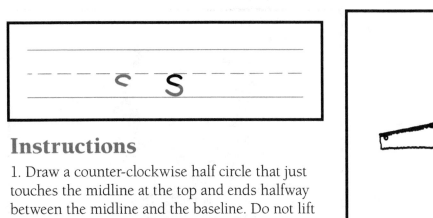

Instructions

1. Draw a counter-clockwise half circle that just touches the midline at the top and ends halfway between the midline and the baseline. Do not lift the pencil from the page.

2. Continue with a clockwise half circle that just touches the baseline at the bottom.

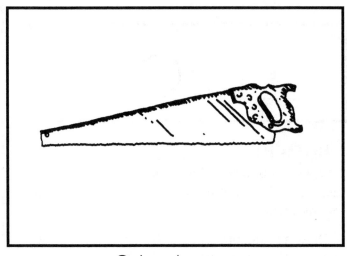

Color the saw.

Trace and write the small letter **s**.

s

Write the word **sniggle.**

Write the sentence **Moses read the commandments**. Don't forget the period.

Provide more practice on the chalkboard or on ruled paper, as needed.

Instructions

1. Beginning a little below the headline, draw a counter-clockwise half circle ending on the midline. Do not lift the pencil from the page.

2. Draw a clockwise half circle from the end of the first stroke that touches the baseline and ends a little above it.

COLOR THE SUN.

Trace and write the capital letter **S**.

Write the word **Samuel.**

Write the sentence **The Lord called Moses to Sinai**. Don't forget the period.

Provide more practice on the chalkboard or on ruled paper, as needed.

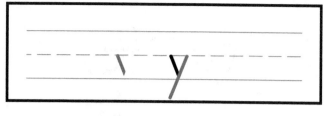

Color the yarn.

Instructions

1. Draw a slanted line left to right from the midline to the baseline.

2. Draw a slanted line right to left from the midline to the descender line. This line should touch the right end of the first slanted line.

Trace and write the small letter **y**.

Write the word **year.**

Write the sentence **Mary yelled at Lyle.** Don't forget the period.

Provide more practice on the chalkboard or on ruled paper, as needed.

62

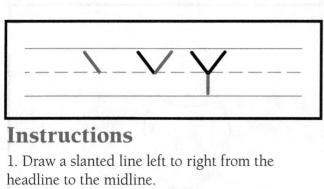

Instructions

1. Draw a slanted line left to right from the headline to the midline.
2. Draw a slanted line right to left from the headline to the end of the first stroke on the midline.
3. Draw a straight line from the midline to the baseline.

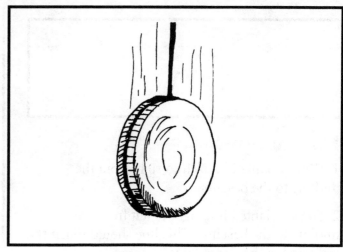

COLOR THE YO-YO.

Trace and write the capital letter **Y**.

Write the word **Yodeling**.

Write the sentence **Ypsilanti is in Michigan**. Don't forget the period.

Provide more practice on the chalkboard or on ruled paper, as needed.

63

Instructions

1. Draw a slanted line left to right from the midline to the baseline.

2. Draw a slanted line right to left from the midline to the baseline. This line should touch the right end of the slanted line.

Color the vase.

Trace and write the small letter **v**.

Write the word **very**.

Write the sentence **Jesus saves everyone who truly believes**. Don't forget the period.

Provide more practice on the chalkboard or on ruled paper, as needed.

COLOR THE VOLCANO.

Instructions

1. Draw a slanted line left to right from the headline to the baseline.

2. Draw a slanted line right to left from the headline to the baseline. This line should touch the right end of the first slanted line.

Trace and write the capital letter **V**.

Write the word **Verse.**

Write the sentence **Volcanoes are very gorgeous.** Don't forget the period.

Provide more practice on the chalkboard or on ruled paper, as needed.

65

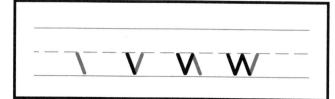

Instructions

1. Draw a slanted line left to right from the midline to the baseline.
2. Draw a slanted line right to left from the midline to the baseline. This line should touch the right end of the first slanted line.
3. Begin where the second stroke began. Draw a slanted line left to right from the midline to the baseline.
4. Draw a slanted line right to left from the midline to the baseline. This line should touch the right end of the third slanted line.

Color the watch.

Trace and write the small letter **w**.

Write the word **woven**.

Write the sentence **Samson went with the jawbone**. Don't forget the period.

Provide more practice on the chalkboard or on ruled paper, as needed.

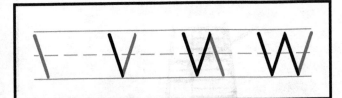

Instructions

1. Draw a slanted line left to right from the headline to the baseline.
2. Draw a slanted line right to left from the headline to the baseline. This line should touch the right end of the first slanted line.
3. Begin where the second stroke began. Draw a slanted line left to right from the headline to the baseline.
4. Draw a slanted line right to left from the headline to the baseline. This line should touch the right end of the third slanted line.

COLOR THE WAGON.

Trace and write the capital letter **W.**

Write the word **Waverly.**

Write the words **When Wanda wove.**

Provide more practice on the chalkboard or on ruled paper, as needed.

67

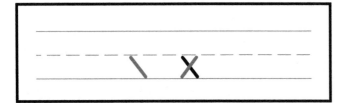

Instructions

1. Draw a slanted line left to right from the midline to the baseline.

2. Draw a slanted line right to left from the midline to the baseline. This line should cross the first slanted line just above the middle.

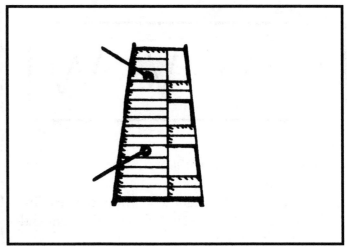

Color the xylophone.

Trace and write the small letter **x**.

Write the word **ax**.

Write the sentence **Did you wax the xylophone?** Don't forget the question mark.

Provide more practice on the chalkboard or on ruled paper, as needed.

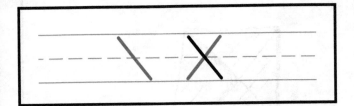

Instructions

1. Draw a slanted line left to right from the headline to the baseline.

2. Draw a slanted line right to left from the headline to the baseline. This line should cross the middle of the first slanted line.

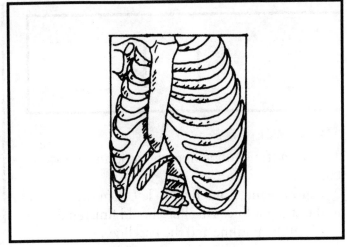

COLOR THE X-RAY.

Trace and write the capital letter **X**.

Write the word **Xylophone**.

Write the sentence **X-rays do not hurt oxen**. Don't forget the period.

Provide more practice on the chalkboard or on ruled paper, as needed.

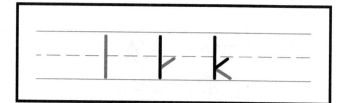

Instructions

1. Draw a straight line from the headline to the baseline.
2. Draw a slanted line right to left from the midline to the straight line. This line should finish halfway between the midline and the baseline.
3. Draw a slanted line left to right from the end of the second line to the baseline.

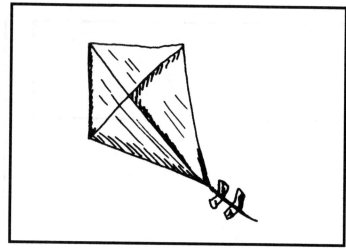

Color the kite.

Trace and write the small letter **k**.

Write the word **knock**.

Write the sentence **Jack picked up a black ax**. Don't forget the period.

Provide more practice on the chalkboard or on ruled paper, as needed.

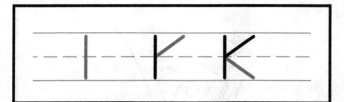

Instructions

1. Draw a straight line from the headline to the baseline.
2. Draw a slanted line right to left from the headline to the midline. The slanted line should end in the middle of the first stroke.
3. Draw a slanted line from the midline to the baseline.

COLOR THE KING.

Trace and write the capital letter **K**.

Write the word **Kentucky.**

Write the sentence **King Karl kicked the volleyball**. Don't forget the period.

Provide more practice on the chalkboard or on ruled paper, as needed.

Instructions

1. Draw a horizontal line on the midline.
2. Draw a slanted line right to left from the midline to the baseline. The slanted line should touch the end of the straight line.
3. Draw a straight line on the baseline. This line should begins where the slanted line ended and should end right under the end of the first straight line.

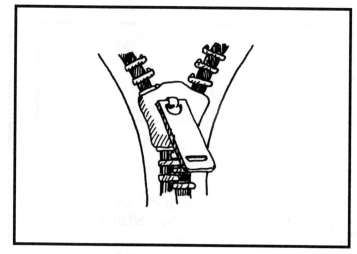

Color the zipper.

Trace and write the small letter **z**.

Write the word **zero**.

Write the sentence **Katy whizzed by the zoo.** Don't forget the period.

Provide more practice on the chalkboard or on ruled paper, as needed.

Instructions

1. Draw a horizontal line on the headline.

2. Draw a slanted line from the headline to the baseline.

3. Draw a straight line on the baseline. This line should end right under the end of the first straight line.

COLOR THE ZEBRA.

Trace and write the capital letter **Z**.

Write the word **Zelotes.**

Write the sentence **Zachariah amazed Judah.** Don't forget the period.

Provide more practice on the chalkboard or on ruled paper, as needed.

73

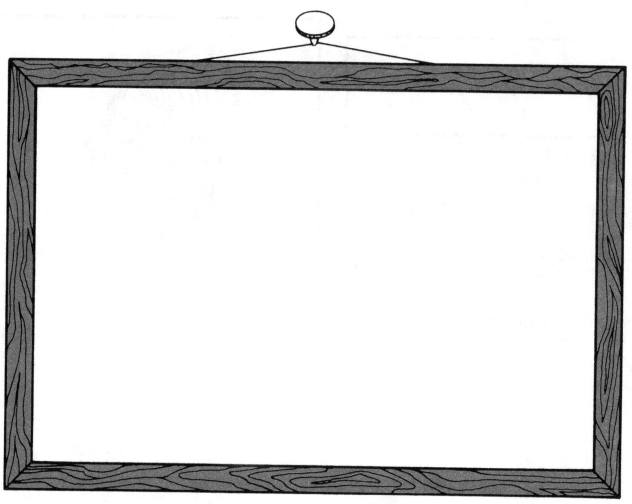

My Phone Number

Draw a picture of someone you would like to talk to on the telephone. Practice writing your phone number.

Help your students evaluate how they are progressing.

How Am I Learning?

Are you ready to write? Do your best work as you copy this sentence.
With a quick jerk, the big fuzzy musk ox pulled the cart into view.

Answer the following questions.   Circle

1. Am I keeping all letters on the baseline?	Yes	No
2. Am I shaping every letter correctly?	Yes	No
3. Am I making each letter the correct height?	Yes	No
4. Am I spacing letters evenly?	Yes	No
5. Am I leaving space between words?	Yes	No
6. Am I capitalizing and using periods or questions marks?	Yes	No
7. Am I leaving extra space between sentences?	Yes	No

Letters I write well:

Letters I need to practice:

Write a letter to Jesus thanking him for His help in teaching you to write. Ask Him to help you try to do well always for the Father's glory. Remember to use periods and question marks.